Voices from September 11th

Lavonne Mueller

APPLAUSE
THEATRE & CINEMA BOOKS

Voices from September 11th
by Lavonne Mueller
Copyright © 2002 by Lavonne Mueller
All rights reserved

Library of Congress Cataloguing-in-Publication Data:
Mueller, Lavonne.
  Voices from September 11th / by Lavonne Mueller.
    p. cm.
  ISBN 1-55783-590-X
  1. September 11 Terrorist Attacks, 2001—Drama. 2. Victims of
  terrorism—Drama. 3. New York (N.Y.)—Drama. I. Title.
  PS3563.U346 V64 2002
  812'.54—dc21

                    2002009221

            British Library Cataloguing-in-Publication Data
            A catalogue record for this book is available from the British
            Library

ISBN: 1-55783-590-X

APPLAUSE THEATRE & CINEMA BOOKS
151 West 46th Street, 8th Floor
New York, NY 10036
Phone: (212) 575-9265
Fax: (646) 562-5852
Email: info@applausepub.com
Internet: www.applausepub.com

SALES & DISTRIBUTION

North America: UK:
HAL LEONARD CORP.   COMBINED BOOK SERVICES LTD.
7777 West Bluemound Road   Units I/K, Paddock Wood Distribution Centre
P. O. Box 13819   Paddock Wood, Tonbridge, Kent TN12 6UU
Milwaukee, WI 53213   Phone: (44) 01892 837171
Phone: (414) 774-3630   Fax: (44) 01892 837272
Fax: (414) 774-3259   United Kingdom
Email: halinfo@halleonard.com
Internet: www.halleonard.com

Characters

Earl, firefighter, age 26

Terry's Father, father of a woman who died at World Trade Center, age 67

Elmore "Torch" Vaughn, baseball player, age 20-something

The Pilot, age 40

Umm, Muslim American woman, age 28, six months pregnant

Doris, game show hostess, age 20-something

Mary Edilia, trucker, age 38

Patoo, Caribbean woman, age late 30s

Cora, high school student, age 17-and-a-half

Jenny, housewife, age 29

Captain Alley Sand, U.S. Army officer, age 32

Fala, Franklin D. Roosevelt's pet dog

Production Notes

For a full evening in the theatre, monologues may be read separately or spliced—part of one monologue intercepting another. There may be an intermission after six monologues or the monologues may be performed without an intermission.

Any six monologues may be performed as a one-act.

Suggestions for Doubling

(Five actors: Three women, two men)

One Actress
Mary Edilia, trucker
Jenny, housewife

One Actress
Doris, game show hostess
Cora, high school student
Captain Alley Sand, U.S. Army officer

One Actress
Umm, Muslim American woman
Patoo, Caribbean woman

One Actor
Fala, Franklin D. Roosevelt's pet dog
Earl, firefighter
Elmore "Torch" Vaughn, baseball player

One Actor
The Pilot
Terry's Father, father of woman who died at World Trade Center

Scenes

One Hundred Days

CHARACTER: Earl, firefighter, age 26

EARL

I was getting my son ready for pre-school. I had just
helped him put his Cookie Monster t-shirt over his arms
when I noticed a bruise by his elbow and was about to
worry myself into thinking that it was something bad
when my wife came running into the bedroom screaming, "Earl! Earl! You won't believe what happened."

My wife had been in the kitchen with our dog, Homer,
and I figured the mutt had pulled one of his stunts.
Like the last one when he dug into a pan of chocolate
cupcakes cooling on the oven rack and got muffin tins
stuck in his jaw for a vet bill of one week's groceries.
"What's Homer done now?"

"We've been attacked." Jenny began to cry. When
Jimmy saw his mother cry, he started to bawl. Then
Homer bounded in and jumped on the new bedspread
that looked like a bed of flowers and wasn't paid for
yet. And I thought right then and there, Jimmy's
bruise is absolutely nothing.

I'm a fireman from Trenton, so I knew I had to jump in my car, race to New York City, and help my brothers.

As I was speeding down the expressway, electric signs kept flashing: "New York City is closed. New York City is closed."

When I got to Chambers Street, scorched police cars and cabs lined the curbs, some with charred paper coffee cups still on their dashboards. I parked my car, wondering if I'd ever see it again. Ash-covered people were frantically running past me. A hunk of the South Tower struck Banker's Trust on Liberty Street. Brooks Brothers on Church Street was set up as a temporary morgue.

I approached the site where the towers had stood. Both towers had fallen. Cots for the wounded were being set up on West Street just opposite where the South Tower had been. A man in a bomb suit, seventy-five layers of Kevlar with metal plates in front, nudged my side as he angled forward. A search dog rode over smoldering rubble in a basket-pulley to get to a spiraling twist of ruins. Gray dust and soot were thick, as if pasted to the air. Steel slabs jutted ten stories high. This was all that was left of sixteen acres, a city of business that even had its own zip codes.

All of Lower Manhattan was on fire.

I ran to a group of firemen with axes. I told them who I was and we all moved into a deep black maw. Charred rubbish rattled on my helmet. We hacked at a pile of fallen doors where a hand protruded from underneath. I stopped to take off my shirt and wrapped it around my nose and mouth. Three of us began to pound away until we liberated a woman who was conscious but terrified. I patted down her singed hair with my hands, and the fireman next to me took off his shirt and gently draped it over her head. She wobbled to a Red Cross nurse.

"Water! Over here. Water!" somebody yelled, the voice thinned by lung smoke.

A New York City Fire Department chaplain, taking off his helmet to give the last rites to the injured, was killed by falling debris.

I stared at the fire and rubbed lip balm under my nose to help kill the stench. Fire had always been the enemy; the red devil, the villain. Ever since I was eight years old and saw poor Bambi driven from the burning forest, I knew I had to be a fireman.

Suddenly, rubble exploded and ripped the helmet off my head. Thick ash swelled in my ears and I couldn't hear. I knew this was an enemy I'd never fought before. This fire would burn for one hundred days.

New York City Fire Department Engine 54 sent out fifteen men to the first call. None returned. Engine 10, Ladder 10, known as 10-and-10, was the firehouse closest to the World Trade Center; they lost four men, their truck, and their building. In just one hour, more people were killed here than at Pearl Harbor.

I helped two policemen carry a woman to the site's basement where a mini-mart was functioning as a triage center. A lab retriever whined at my feet, his eyes blurry from smoke, his handler strapping a camera around his neck so the dog could plunder the underworld and give the topside some needed pictures. I took a water bottle from my pocket, leaned over and flushed his eyes, then watched him scratch into a black opening just large enough for his belly. Then he disappeared into the bowels of wreckage.

I picked up an air mask from the grime with twenty minutes of oxygen left on it, then shared nozzle time with other firefighters, helping them drag hoses over shattered desks, bookcases, mountains of computer paper, thick manuals, squashed tires, girders, carpets, charred hooks and ladders, and body parts. The smell of decay, like rotten cheese, rose from the ground that was a suppurating wound. Trees were covered with bits of memos, tax forms, keys, envelopes, shoe soles, calendar pads, a British driver's license, a Deutsche Bank ID card, clean white teeth...and...a watch still ticking.

Flames consumed everything…even the concrete burned …even the birds were on fire.

I picked up a white pigeon from the boiling crud—its wings crusted with ash, silt, and glass shards. Its life smoked out. And I thought, as I looked at the scorched creature in my hand: No, this isn't a pigeon. It's a dove. And America's not blessed with peace anymore.

Windows on the World

CHARACTER: Terry's Father, father of a woman who died at the World Trade Center, age 67

*(At rise: **Terry's Father** holds a lady's hairbrush)*

TERRY'S FATHER

My daughter, Terry, worked at the Windows on the World Restaurant on the 107th floor. A fifty-eight-second elevator ride to the top. A ninety-mile view covering three states.

Tuesday was supposed to be her day off, but somebody got sick and being the kind of person she is, Terry volunteered to go in. I never want to know who was sick.

I know what I was doing in Chicago that morning when my only child was serving little melon balls and scrambled eggs topped off with sprigs of parsley to a group of Wall Street brokers. I had just turned off the Cream of Wheat my wife Betty likes and the butter patty was melting slowly on top—little yellow streaks shooting into thick creamy whiteness. After I scooped the first spoonful from the pan, I heard Betty scream from the living room. We don't eat Cream of Wheat anymore.

I taught Terry how to cook. She was only eight years old when I showed her how to carve flowers out of radishes. For her birthday she always wanted fancy mixing bowls. One Christmas she got a doll and immediately buried it in our backyard. When she was a teen and going out on dates, she smelled of nougat and waffles and didn't have to spend money on perfume.

My father was a chef and his father before him.

I was an Army cook. In Korea. Terry always bragged to her kids and friends about me being a nineteen-year-old company cook at Fort Hood when Elvis was a raw recruit. Terry made me tell everybody how he looked like all the other guys. Crew cut. Fatigues. He used to polish his brass better than any of them. But what I remember best from those days was when Elvis pulled KP. That's right, he pulled Kitchen Police just like the rest. When Terry was little and liked to make a mess in the kitchen with greasy pans on the kitchen table, I always told her—If Elvis can clean up, you can, too. It pretty much worked back then. Now… well…I'd give anything to wash any dish or pan she ever used.

My daughter was good at carving ice for centerpieces. Up there in that restaurant in the sky, you could see her ice sculptures of doves and butterflies. Looking at the rubble now, which once was a great building that she was so proud to work in, I remember my Uncle

Joe who's a detective and how he always said that the first moments are never the right ones. And that is true because after some weeks have gone by, I'm no longer tortured by a vision of her being trapped. I now imagine Terry flying out those windows on the world and melting like one of her ice-birds into the warm blanket of the sky.

Coming here to Ground Zero...was hard for my wife and me. You notice that people tend to whisper. I brought Terry's hairbrush for a DNA sample. She used this brush on her hair the morning she went to work. I never thought I'd be carrying it to someplace like this...and I can't help but think about long ago when times were innocent and our ancestors buried their loved ones outside the kitchen window. Now, remains are recovered, forensics people give them an identification number, cut away a small sample, and extract DNA. The sample is frozen and packed and shipped to a lab for genetic fingerprints that are a long line of numbers plotted into wavy graphs. It's hard to think of my daughter being nothing but a wavy graph...not a smiling face with wavy hair.

Right over there, President Bush took a bullhorn from the ground and shouted to firemen, "I can hear you. The rest of the world hears you. And the people who knocked these buildings down will hear all of us soon."

Some scam artists tried to sell soil from this area. Boasting it was sacred and all. But Mayor Giuliani stopped all that by assuring families he would provide a proper urn for us. In my opinion, that alone justified *Time* magazine making Giuliani Man of the Year. But the Mayor couldn't stop those vendors who sold World Trade Center snow globes from last year. It's hard to hate anybody, though, for bad taste.

It's funny the things you think of...in grief. I remember that man called the "human fly" who clamped devices that he designed on his feet and began his three-and-a-half hour ascent of the World Trade Center in 1977. That guy was charged with criminal trespassing, but I wish he was climbing on September 11th and got to the 107th floor to carry my daughter down to safety.

And...why couldn't a copter land on the roof? In 1993, a chopper pilot helped rescue twenty-eight people from the roof of the north tower after a bomb exploded in the Trade Center's basement... the roof doors were locked that day, too, but police were able to use tools to break open the doors. Why...why couldn't they break down the roof doors this time?

A lot of architects and engineers are saying it's not practical to design structures to avoid the impact of airplanes...that skyscrapers are an American symbol. But the skyscraper for me is not a sign of progress and wealth…but a symbol of loss and human suffering. The Towers might be gone, but it's the people left behind who have to stand tall.

But how can I be really bitter when I see little kids draw blue chalk flowers on the sidewalk in a project called The Path of Remembrance for those who died September 11th. Four thousand chalk flowers wound from Michigan Avenue to the lake…not too far from where my wife and I live and where Terry grew up in Chicago. Betty and I went out and each drew a rose bud—ours looked more like the sugary rose buds that Terry liked to make out of icing. Then we stared at the pale pink chalk when we were done…knowing that chalk is about as fleeting and delicate as life itself.

My old dad was a World War II sailor who lost some of his good buddies on the *Arizona*. Dad talked about l,177 lives that rest at the bottom of the water. And now I think on nearly 3,000 people who rest at the bottom of vaporized concrete.

(A beat)

Some of you might have read the paragraph about Terry in *The New York Times*…in their "Portraits of Grief" column. The *Times* called us up to talk about Terry and I said for them to just publish her recipe for cranberry muffins and put her name, date of birth and death under it. I understand people all over the

world bake those muffins as a kind of memorial. I
like that tribute better than the one proposed by an
architect who wants to rebuild the two towers and
put a pit between them that's 911-feet deep.

We didn't take any money, either. The Red Cross
called us, but we said thanks but no thanks. It was
kind of folks to contribute. We just can't stand the
idea of receiving money for the worst thing that ever
happened to us. And we definitely don't want to get
involved in more agony—with the Red Cross using 9-
11 money for unrelated projects—and people like us
accused of demanding big profits for their tragedy.

A lot of times, somebody will ask me if I'm angry that
the USA gives rations to Afghanistan. But the people
over there that did the killing aren't the destitute
ones. No, killers always get themselves plenty to eat.
I know my daughter would like the fact that thirty-
seven thousand bright yellow food packages are
being dropped for the poor and hungry people who
probably never even saw Osama bin Laden in their
whole lives. I wouldn't want some Afghan dad to go
through what I am by losing a starving child. And
wouldn't Elvis like it that peanut butter is included
in those humanitarian drops? Yes, my Terry always
knew that food was peace.

Twelve Stars Missing

CHARACTER: Elmore "Torch" Vaughn, baseball player, age 20-something

ELMORE

I've been playing baseball since I was eight years old. I'm on the Paterson Outlooks, my hometown team, which is well-known in New Jersey. Like our Mayor always says, our games keep the hoodlums off the street.

The morning of September 11th, Dad and I went over to Brunswick to watch Moe, my brother, at an early practice for the last day of his job of carrying bats. Moe was leaving the next day for the major leagues—to be a vendor at Yankee Stadium. That was Moe's idea of slowly working himself up to be a manager some day.

Tuesdays are my day off from my regular job as a veterinarian's assistant. Just the day before, I had helped finish a C-section on a diabetic tabby. I was feeling good that morning and looking forward to a game that night. The weather was clear and crisp and Moe was doing his job, putting the bats down nicely when somebody came running onto the field yelling, "We're at war! New York's been hit." We were in a state of shock, deciding if we should believe him or not. Moe came running over and we took off for the house where we saw the awful truth on TV. All Dad said was that his father was listening to the Bears play the Cardinals on December 7, 1941 when the Japanese attacked Pearl Harbor.

That night, the Paterson Outlooks decided not to play out of respect for the victims of the Twin Towers. In fact, we really didn't know when to start up again. The whole country was depressed. There were no sports going on anywhere. Guys that never spent a weekend without a can of Bud and a baseball game on TV were staring at CNN.

Some of my teammates hopped on down to the local hospital to give blood. Other guys sent checks to the Red Cross. I thought about joining up, but our manager, Everett Birdie, called us all together and read a letter that President Roosevelt wrote during the Second World War called a green-light letter that was sent to baseball commissioner, Kenesaw Mountain Landis: "It would be best for the country to keep baseball going. These players are a definite recreational asset to at least 20 million of their fellow citizens, and that in my judgment is thoroughly worthwhile." That letter made me proud.

On our first game of September 30th, the whole team was edgy. It didn't help that a group of Paterson

Baptists were out by our hand-operated scoreboard that day chanting "USA, USA, Jesus is standing at the home plate for USA." Season ticket holders yelled for me to get my front foot out so I could put my butt into the game. All that caused me to squeeze the bat too hard. The pressure shot right up my body till even my eyebrows went stiff. Then I crowded the plate, wrecking any kind of reaction time. The pitcher was looking at me like I was a wild wolf that had just come through his bedroom window. It was easy for him to draw me out to hit a wide one. I swung too soon and pulled the ball foul. I had taken to smoking for my nerves and just before I came up to bat, I sneaked a puff and hid a flaming butt in my belt loop. When I finally struck out, I also caught on fire. That's how I got the nickname "Torch."

With Moe being hired as a vendor in the Big Leagues hawking peanuts and dogs for the Yankees, Dad and I were excited about the Yankees going for the World Series again—especially in the days after September 11th. Now there was a spot of cheer and hope among a lot of shell-shocked New Yorkers. And we all admired Joe Torre who could bring tears to our eyes—good old Yankee Joe from Brooklyn's Avenue T. At the games, Joe went out shaking hands and hugging kids who lost their fathers in the World Trade Center. A pregnant widow held Joe's hand. "The tragedy left us feeling so helpless," Torre said, "that it feels good to touch people who need something to hold on to." And Joe

Torre held on tight to a picture of a firefighting father that a five-year-old kid gave him.

Moe called one day to tell us that President Bush himself was coming to Yankee Stadium to cheer on the country and throw out the first ball. He'd heard it from one of the ground crew whose sister was married to the cousin of a guy who was the President's barber. If Dad and I wanted to see him, Moe could get us in.

Did we want to see the President of our country?!

The Outlooks weren't playing for a few days, so Dad and me got a midnight Greyhound express from Paterson to New York City. Mom packed fried mush, hominy pudding, her famous tapioca, fist-sized biscuits, and pumpkin butter. But I was so excited I couldn't eat.

Moe met us at the bus station and took us to his one-room apartment in the Bronx. Moe told me to suit up. If I wanted to get close to the Commander in Chief, I had to wear a hat and vest and sell hot dogs with him, though he warned me I would be working in a place as big as that Roman Coliseum I'd read about in Miss Stoppelmoor's history class, and would probably end up with gladiator-type blisters all over my feet. If I were lucky, the President would buy something from me.

Moe sat me on an old sofa with its insides dragging on the floor and told me not to embarrass him if I did get lucky. "Be sure and call him sir," he said. Then we each drank a glass of water from an old Cracker Jack box because Moe never washed glasses.

We got to Yankee Stadium early. There were hundreds of buses lined up outside. I just stood in awe of the most important piece of property in the whole world.

The bleachers were jammed but Dad was able to squeeze into a spot.

It was like all of New York was there, like a neighborhood trying to be normal again. I looked down, past a group of women with t-shirts that said: "USA All The Way Yankees." The bases looked so white and clean.

It was the Yankees against the Arizona Diamondbacks. All the players, even the umps, wore American flag patches.

Security was tight. Fans had to walk through metal detectors. Moe and I lifted our arms to be checked. Police used a hand-operated wand over each and every one of our hot dogs. The elevators were closed until the middle of the eighth inning. No planes were permitted to fly overhead.

Moe showed me how to walk carrying the vending tray on my hip, keeping my right arm clear for handing out franks and taking money. Then he showed me the President's box seat. We had to sell all the FBI officers hot dogs before they let us touch the seat for luck.

Fans hollered for service. I was working both hands. Moe was even putting his head and shoulders into the job, pushing along paper cups of Coke with his chin. He could pitch a bag of peanuts over fifty rows. Moe thought vendors had to have "muscle memory" like a ball player and build themselves up to the point where the muscles know how to act automatically. "Good vendors oughta have their own baseball cards," he said, "because this is really their stadium—baseball players come and go."

The place got so packed, fans had to hold hot dogs over their heads to side-step into a seat. Spill-over crowds were standing in the ramps. A scuffle broke out between a shirt saying: "I Ate 1,000 Hot Dogs For USA" and a red baseball hat with the words: "D-Backs For America." Thanks to the rough-housing, I got a precious piece of broken bleacher to take home.

Soon there was a proclaimed silence to mourn the victims of September 11th. Over the infield's big screen were the words: "USA Fears Nothing. Play Ball."

The President came out of the Yankees' dugout wearing a blue New York Fire Department jacket. He paused, considered the ball, then whipped one in for a strike like he was showing bin Laden how we do things in America. Fifty-seven thousand people chanted: USA, USA, USA. Over center field, a ripped and ash-covered flag from the Twin Towers was flying with twelve stars missing.

I never did get to sell a hot dog or Coke to the President that day. He left in the third inning. The Yankees won the game 2-l, and all I could do was just sit there in the stands and watch the flag with twelve stars missing. And I thought...it's wonderful how baseball is about so many things beside baseball.

I still have that scrap of wood from Yankee Stadium. Here, you can touch it.

The Pilot

CHARACTER: The Pilot, age 40

(A pilot comes on stage. He takes off his cap and holds it in his hand.)

THE PILOT

I've been flying since I was nine. I took out across pea patches and corn fields in a rig I built myself out of an orange crate and my sister's roller skates. Used to get airsick so I flew with a bucket between my legs. In high school, I asked for the old man's plane the way other kids asked to use the car.

On September 11th I was flying out of Los Angeles's LAX Airport to New York's Kennedy. It was an early flight with over one hundred people on my 727. We had been airborne for only forty minutes. The wind was strong...and flying that bobbing 727 in turbulence was like dancing with a hippopotamus. I had just switched on the seat belt sign and was feeling the awe of the atmosphere, when I got a radio command: "Land! Land immediately at the nearest airport." I tried to ask questions...tried to get explanations...but the ground controller ordered: "Land! Right now!"

I made contact with an airport in Albuquerque, New Mexico, and got clearance. I moved down smoothly as the engines screamed and the ground came up to meet me. A mechanic ran out to the tarmac waving day-glo wands that directed me to an area where three other planes were on hold. I was given the news about the Twin Towers and had to tell the passengers and crew. One elderly lady in first class started screaming and we got a doctor in to sedate her. The woman's daughter had just begun a new job at the World Trade Center.

As details filtered in, I discovered that I knew two of the crew who died when those planes slammed into the Towers and the Pentagon. In this business, crews are like family and we suffer greatly when one of us is injured or killed. I felt like the screaming lady in first class, only my screams were silent.

My dad always said, "Anybody who chooses to fly has to love birds." And I think that's true. A bird knows all the moods of the sky. Just like us. There's a remoteness from earthly worries up there. Pure pleasure and ease that both man and bird can appreciate. I often watch a robin glide, put its nose down to gain forward speed, climb, loop, spin. But looking at a hundred flights means there are also a hundred landings. That bird—just like a pilot—has to get back down. One way or the other. Now, when I watch a sparrow take off, I only think about the "coming down." An airplane digs its own grave.

In my youth, it was a more innocent time. I had my own little two-seater. My white Scottie, Buster, would sit on the right wing until I started up the engine. Then he'd jump down and run behind me like any family mutt chasing after a car...his warm friendly eyes following me up...up...into the clouds.

Today, there are no warm friendly eyes. Passengers look straight ahead with steely eyes, unsmiling and suspicious.

And my spirits drop when I find my plane has mostly women and children aboard. If we're hijacked and have an all-out fight, women and children will be of little help.

The passengers have a new game—trying to identify the air marshals who have made a great effort to blend in. Even I'm not told their seat locations until shortly before takeoff.

Our cockpit door has been reinforced with a steel bar across it, but that didn't stop a man recently from busting over it with his head.

In the past, flight attendants would hand out decks of cards to travelers. In the good old days, I'd walk back to the cabin and see people playing chess. Sometimes I'd even move a chess piece as I walked by...hearing laughter through the aisles. But there's not that kind of fraternizing any more. I'm all alone up front with just my co-pilot and the engineer...shooting through the atmosphere in something that could very easily be a weapon. The dog on my right wing isn't my white Scottie anymore but the black dog of death.

Voices from September 11th

Umm

CHARACTER: Umm, Muslim American woman, age 28, six months pregnant

*(**Umm** holds a menu.)*

UMM

I was taking my morning shower before going to work at Kulchi Palace, a restaurant my husband Rashid and I own in Akron. We serve mostly Afghan food—mountain tea, hot chocolate, coffee, sweet biscuits called *kulchi*, roast lamb, rice, couscous, naan, milk pudding. I was going in early because I had ordered some special cakes from a friend of my cousin, Hajera, which were supposed to display the words *ahlan wa-sallan* (you are welcome) in icing on the top, something I thought would be fanciful for desert. I like to take a long relaxing hot shower every morning, especially now that I'm pregnant—it's like I'm showering for two. And perhaps it goes back to the *hammams*, the popular baths of my native country, where it's such a simple joy in washing oneself. Rashid knows that I love to linger and daydream, scrub the new orb of my pregnant belly. So when he pounded on the door, interrupting my shower, I knew something was wrong.

He pressed his head against the shower door and groaned. I saw his gold tooth through the soapy fogged glass. "Umm...Umm...you must come out." It sounded like some Imam's *fatwa*.

When he told me about the World Trade Center, the first thing I said was, "Please, Allah, don't let it be a Muslim."

Rashid leaned over the stove and tried to brew tea so we could calm ourselves. Because we now knew. The pilots who flew the planes were Muslims.

It's not uncommon for us to have hot yogurt soup for breakfast. Some sweet black olives. Creamy feta cheese. Flat bread. But that morning, we only had tea.

Then the phone began to ring. One cousin after the other. My mother in New Jersey. All of them crying, "What are we going to do? Where should we go?"

"We're going nowhere," said Rashid. He poured tea in two tulip-shaped glasses with three lumps of sugar for each. "Don't go out. Send a neighbor for food." Dizzy with grief, he held the tea glasses on a server, like a tea-carrier in a Kabul bazaar, drinks swaying at incredible angles.

Kulchi Palace was closed, of course, on September 11th and for weeks afterwards. And someone, thinking themselves patriotic—and believing we were sleeper-agents for bin Laden—threw a brick in the front window on September 12th. Some time later, "killer" was scribbled on the front door. When I walked on the street, boys yelled, "Scheherazade, go back where you belong." My cousin, Nazifa, emailed me that she had to remove her *hijab*, her head covering, even after she successfully passed the metal detector when she entered the Sears Tower in Chicago. Nazifa is traditional, and there is great shame in removing your *hijab*, especially in front of men. Rashid could only mutter an old Afghanistan saying, "When you can't beat the donkey, beat the saddle."

My family came to America from Afghanistan shortly after the Russians invaded in 1979. I was only six years old. My mother and father and I were able to come over because my mother's sister, Laili, sponsored us. Aunt Laili had married an American Arab and quickly became a U.S. citizen, too. My mother and father worked in Aunt Laili's restaurant, Kandahar House, and when father died four years ago, mother continued working there right up to September 11th. But after that tragic Tuesday, people began canceling retirement dinners, weddings and engagement ceremonies, birthday parties and Sunday brunches. Major annual Islamic conventions were called off. Kandahar House closed six months later. Aunt Laili and Uncle Javed got jobs at Easy Stop, a fast food restaurant where they now cook in a closed kitchen area so no one can see them.

Rashid is just your average Tom-Dick-Mohammad who goes to the mosque to pray without paying any attention to politics. He's lived in Akron all his life and is as American as anyone. And after I married him, I became a citizen, too. We both went to Ohio State. We have no relatives who are Taliban. My cousin, Asem, is fighting with the Northern Alliance, alongside U.S. troops. My Uncle Jamal died in Qara-Bach, shot by the Al Qaeda.

(A beat.)

And remember…four hundred Muslims lost their lives in the World Trade Center.

I guess I always knew I was different. Even from age six, when I first came to this country. And it wasn't just the dark tint of my skin. In those long ago times before mosques were allowed to use loudspeakers, my mother spoke of napping beside the family farm animals while her mother gossiped with women in *burqas* the color of sunflowers. My uncles were turbaned men on horseback, who worked in a pony market. And unlike Americans, I ate on the floor—even in Ohio—with the whole family, over bean and almond soup, baked lamb with sumac. I had Farsi-American dictionaries on my bookshelf, wore nomad bracelets. My mother never wore the veil, nor did any of my sisters. Mother always said that when females go on the Hajj to Mecca, they are required *not* to cover their faces. That, she felt, proves her point. So over the years, all I did was cover my hair…in Kabul, and in Akron, too.

Kulchi Palace opened again in November. Fifty Christian churches volunteered to patrol mosques, Islamic schools, and even restaurants like Kulchi Palace.

But it's the little things that bother me. I worry for myself…for my husband…for my baby that will soon arrive…especially when a customer says suspiciously, "Are you a born American or a paper one? Why do you people all come over here and try to get our money?" So Rashid and I found ourselves deciding to adapt the menu. After September 11th, costs had to be reconsidered. Everyone would be watching our ethnic food. If we charged too much, customers wouldn't come. If we charged too little, they would think our food wasn't quality. If we charged the right amount by Akron standards, people would be disappointed after having their hopes raised by the promise of Afghan poverty. So Rashid and I are lacing fast foods into our staples…meat loaf kibbeh…hot dogs rizz…macaroni and Laban cheese. We reason that fast foods for Americans are more of a tradition than the Muslim veil. We just copied the exact prices from the Sandusky Deli across the street…hoping now…no one will be angry. Hoping…if people can't beat the donkey, maybe they won't beat the saddle.

Game Show

CHARACTER: Doris, game show hostess, age 20-something

*(At rise: **Doris** comes on stage. She wears a small white face mask over her hair like sunglasses.)*

DORIS

You don't expect a catastrophe when you're eating an onion bagel at a little Greek coffee shop on 72nd and Amsterdam Avenue. It was 8:45 in the morning and I'd just put an extra creamer in my coffee, something I don't indulge in very often. Now that I think back over the years, two of anything tend to bring me bad luck. Once I got burned in a suntanning booth on both my legs. This time…two would mean something much more scary. And I remember the fat old guy next to me yelling his head off when he answered his cell phone, bellowing out over his hash browns that his wife said the World Trade Center got hit. Nobody believed him. By the time I finished my bagel, there was another hit. Some people don't like to sit in any auditorium seat that's number thirteen. Me…I don't sit in two anymore.

I'm a game show hostess. As these times become more and more edgy, I not only feel sad and sometimes scared, but I also worry about my job. I certainly don't mean to take away from the tragedy of all those poor people who died. That's the main horror. But people are getting laid off right and left with the government saying eighty thousand jobs will be lost by the end of the year. Cutbacks by advertisers have already depressed the economy with people like General Motors replacing their hard-sell messages with only a few select feel-good ads. My girlfriend lost her job as a stew on United, even though she spent her own money for self-defense classes at Sharkey's Karate Studio in Queens because the State Department urged people to be aware of terrorists. And a couple of my cousins don't sell luggage at Macy's anymore with the government extending unemployment for thirty-nine weeks. The U.S. Mint has a surplus of coins because people are emptying their piggy banks during these hard times and now the Mint's laying off 357 workers because there's a drop in demand for new coins. Not that my own job is what you call the greatest in the world. It pays the bills, of course, and it helps a little that the President ordered everybody to start spending. "Go shop," said our Commander in Chief. I never thought anybody would have to order me to do that. But...since it's a mandate, like having to get your teeth cleaned every six months, I feel...where's the fun ...where's the scandal of spending thousands of dollars on a Cartier tank watch or a Christian Dior chiffon blouse that has to be in simple black for soothing reasons? I had to throw out all my camouflage t-shirts since that's taboo, though cargo pants are probably still going to be OK.

The producers picked up on patriotic spending real fast, and got a lot of very expensive prizes for our contestants; stuff like snow blowers, cashmere opera coats, new kitchens, home entertainment centers, and diamond bracelets. People were lucky to win louver curtains, maybe a door extender, or a couple of swivel overhead lights before. The new high profile loot, however, is good publicity and good business. It also creates good hysteria, too. Which I have to deal with…all because prize-hysteria helps combat national depression, according to the latest PR.

I usually get a lot of fan mail. But with the anthrax scare, I can't read any of my letters at the studio in spite of what the President himself said quite reassuringly to the press, "I don't have anthrax." That didn't stop our largest elected body, the House of Representatives, to shut down because of scattered spores. My grandpa told me that Buckingham Palace received nine direct hits during the London Blitz and all those ancient royals stood their ground, so why can't we? All you have to do is be alert and vigilant.

(She tugs at her face mask.)

Simple little masks like this cut the risk.

(Now she pulls it down around her neck.)

I also know enough when I'm home to put my mail in the microwave or iron it. A lot of my friends think it's a really trendy thing to do. Still, spores were found in many of the news offices and even at the New York Post Office on Sixth Avenue at 48th Street. I have a cousin who got her nose swabbed and took Cipro. Cipro gave her migraines and broke up her engagement. One other really bad thing about all this is that the metal-band group, Anthrax, is having a hard time dealing with their name. But they refuse to change it. I really admire that.

Nothing...absolutely nothing is the same since September 11th. I have friends who have to have phone-therapy just to go to their office on the twentieth floor. And you can hardly find a salad bar because people are eating more comfort food. The Concorde is serving their dinners with plastic cutlery. There's even a yellow stripe on the floor that you can't cross—right behind the driver's seat on all Greyhound buses. Most of the drivers have pepper spray. There are no waiting lines for the cable cars in San Francisco since most people think the Golden Gate Bridge will go next. And all the women journalists in this studio who head off to Afghanistan to report the news have to dye their slinky blond hair dark brown and wear an ugly head scarf. Not that there aren't some bright spots…like the dry cleaner down the street that offers free flag pressing.

The American Heritage College Dictionary entered "9-11" (it's between "nine days wonder" and "ninepin") into its pages. And the sale of lipstick has gone way up because women still want to enjoy simple pleasures like bright lips. Sometimes you just have to ask yourself, "Where is Dick Cheney?" After all, we're paying for a Vice President.

You may think being a game show hostess is glamorous. Well, it's not. Just hard work. Not to mention the danger. But I get five free wigs for the show and residuals. Even Judy Garland didn't get residuals for *The Wizard of Oz.* And I have national TV coverage, of course, and then all the interesting men you meet who have money. But having said that, I can't help but know that some of those rich men probably worked at one of the Towers…maybe bought bread at the bakery in the Trade Center's underground mall to bring home. Thinking that, I know my life isn't so bad.

I've gone through everything on the way up. I've been draped on top of a block-high bowl of pudding with my circulation cut off by a strawberry strapped on my stomach that was wider than a truck. I once wore a gold-painted headband for three months on tour and broke out with a scalp rash that took three penicillin shots to kill. I've babbled myself into stupors on talk shows. And, I suspect, kissed every decrepit man thirty and older in the business.

(She points to a large gambling wheel offstage.)

That thing over there is the trading wheel. It's perfectly honest. It cost over $500,000...complete with cheat-filters. I spin it...

(She mimes spinning the wheel.)

...and if you guess the number it stops on, you could win something fabulous. With the new prizes we give, you can see why the "cattle" go crazy. That's what we call contestants—cattle. I mean even cultivated people go crazy. Ones that use tinned white asparagus in their soup and eat at places that have opera on the jukebox. Even people who eat beluga caviar... and nail Italian landscapes on their living room wall, and call Detroit "De Trois." They might not serve rat-trap cheese and Ritz Crackers at their parties, but I'll tell you, strictly in parentheses, when it comes to getting something for free, they act no better than anybody else.

Now I'm going to tell you something the producers don't want to get out. The audience doesn't like to see a person win too many prizes. When a contestant goes beyond, say, a fifty thousand dollar value, the audience will turn against him or her. Then there can be some unpleasant hissing and cat-calls. I always say, if you play with human emotions, then you deal with certain human consequences. And I have a conscience. I might have lost a lotta things over the years, but I still got a conscience.

We even have a buzzer-lock on our restroom doors. Losers used to go in there and write on the walls and stop up the sinks.

Someday, I'm leaving this racket to get married. And I keep wondering when I'll meet somebody. Everybody gets married, even oddballs, girls with thin hair, real old people. But I haven't met a guy yet I'd want to spend my life with. I once went with a guy who lived across the street from the World Trade Center and had a pacemaker in his chest. Dennis. He was only twenty-four and it's rare for a person of that age to have a pacemaker. And when we kissed, sometimes I'd hear it whirrrrrr. I could look out his bedroom window and the World Trade Center was so close that I could see one tower hiding behind the other one. At that time, of course, the towers didn't scare me but what did scare me was being afraid that Dennis would die on me and I always thought how embarrassing it would all be if he just…you know…stopped whirrrrring… when we were…you know. It would kill my parents to have that kind of story circulating in Moline. The funny thing is, I really liked the guy—aside from the pacemaker. He was very sensitive. Probably the most sensitive guy I've even known. Maybe his affliction had an influence on him. They say that's sometimes the case.

Though the poor guy wasn't real sophisticated. He took me to this fancy restaurant that was advertised as French cuisine but there was catsup on the table. Not that it bothered me all that much. And I want to be clear on this issue—he wasn't disfigured. Just a slight "swelling" or bump on his upper chest and except for that he had a really good bod. The doctor told him he could do anything the average ordinary twenty-four-year-old man could do, including gutting animals, dirty wrestling, slam dancing. But I never felt comfortable with Dennis and a guy picks that up right away. You can't hide that kind of deceit. So eventually we just drifted apart. But I heard just recently from a friend that Dennis had to be evacuated from his apartment and now there's asbestos and smoke all over his furniture, walls, and inside his closets. They say Dennis walks around in clothes he calls "insurance chic." Now and then I do wonder if he's moved someplace out west like Utah where buildings aren't so high and maybe he has a cowgirl next to him who doesn't mind the whirrrrrring.

All my friends are dating firemen. Heroes are considered a good catch these days—big brute-strength guys you'd never find wearing mesh step-in sandals on the beach. I've been occasionally seeing this hunk from a fire station near my apartment. He makes coffee the way cowboys do—boiling the grounds and water in a pot and handing it out piping hot to all his buddies at Ground Zero. His mother and a group of her lady friends from his hometown of White Fish, Montana, just flew in to New York City to show moral support. That's the kind of close-knit family he comes from.

It's amazing how movies go for horror after 9-11. I guess imaginary terror doesn't look so bad considering what we all just went through. My granddad said that after Pearl Harbor, people went to see Frankenstein. People like to scream in safety.

(A beat.)

Well, the sponsors finally got the audience reaction they wanted. Top ratings for our show. But sometimes I'd like the sponsors to be in on the outbursts I put up with. It's no fun having your ribs punched by an overly excited contestant who's just won a Toyota Avalon, be it a patriotic punch or not. Even the Dallas Cheerleaders don't have to put up with stuff like that.

Well, there's the warning light. In five seconds, I'm on camera. I just got to keep telling myself that nothing's more American and patriotic than winning something.

(She counts slowly to "five.")

Ladies and Gentlemen, your game of games!

(She mimes spinning the gambling wheel, then quickly pulls her face mask over her mouth and nose and hovers over the audience, her hands protecting her vital organs. Screams are heard from the audience as the stage goes dark.)

1.3 Million Miles

CHARACTER: Mary Edilia, trucker, age 38

MARY EDILIA

See the American flag flying from my cab window? I was one of the first truckers to put Old Glory on my rig in these parts. Yep, from that very day now called Black Tuesday.

Since September 11th, I've been pulled over and inspected by troopers wearing M-16s and gas masks strapped to their calves.

I like to think of myself as the "first lady" of the road. All of this state is Lincoln Land. I survey real history here in cab number 88 with "Mary Edilia" painted on both doors. Mary, of course, is my name as well as the better half of Abraham Lincoln. Not to mention I'm the only lady truck driver for APC—Abe's Potato Chip Company. Right now they just came out with a potato chip in the shape of the Statue of Liberty's crown. But I'm better out here on the road. Like today, for example. I just tool along this interstate and it's like being Lincoln's kin. Inside the APC Factory was suffocating. Boring. Nothing's gonna barrel at you around a wide curve.

All the talk these days about the Taliban and Afghans make me think about this Arab guy I used to date. Bahiaddin Ali Faris Ketsaraa Abdul Chucheep. I called him Dul for short. He worked in a Taco Bell at the I-55 Truck Plaza, and he always gave me free coffee even before we started going out. Dul was really nice for an Arab. He didn't wear any headdress with tassels. You know, pretty ordinary. He did have a "prayer bump" just below his hairline from pressing his forehead to the ground in pious meditation. And occasionally I'd get aggravated with the "Mecca indicator" on the ceiling of his Honda. We'd go for a simple drive in the country and this fancy compass gadget kept reminding us which way to bow our heads in prayer when Dul didn't even have an automatic shift. Dul was sweet, though. He gave me a tape of Bluegrass II for my birthday. But with all that's going on in our country right now, he's not at Taco Bell anymore, although he was applying for citizenship and loved America and really believed in the United Nations.

My daughters were freaked out 'cause of his harem. What's so bad about that? When my cousin went into the convent last Easter, everybody thought that was great. What's the difference? There's respect in a harem just like in a convent. Those harem women don't get hit on by any old Dervish like we do by every man and tri-sexual hanging around. Harem women are secluded so men don't gawk at them. Dul said it's a good thing the sun is female or even daylight wouldn't be allowed inside the women's quarters.

Did you know Arab men make the coffee? In the Kingdom, coffee making is the exclusive duty of the male. Dul had a coffee pot with coconut fibers in the spout to keep down the grounds. When I went to his place, he always gave me refills in accordance with the sacred number three. So tell that to all our fancy liberated women slaving away on Mr. Coffee for their bosses. Sometimes those macho guys can surprise you.

Once Dul cooked for me. Everything was very clean. No mud on the food. Melon seeds. Saffron grapes. Fava beans. We used our right hand to scoop up food—the native way. For dessert we snacked on sheep eyes and cracked small Turkish pistachios. He told me about his mother, how she always made desert pudding with coarse sugar and how it took a couple of years to make because Arabs don't have a Christian preoccupation with time like we do. Sometimes he'd sing desert love songs in my ear and smoke amber-perfumed cigarettes stamped with his family crest. Having seen *Lawrence of Arabia* seven times, I know about those things.

Well, that's all in the past. Dul just disappeared after September 11th. Maybe he had to go back to his own country. Maybe he's afraid to try and be an American now.

I have a cell phone to keep me company.

(She holds up the cell phone.)

Of course, cell phones have a new image after September 11th. It gets lonely on the road so I call my daughters from time to time. Their voices are bright rays of sunshine alongside this everlasting yellow striped line, guiding me over bumps and ruts. 'Course any time now that my girls call me, my heart skips a lot of beats 'cause I think right away of those poor people calling their loved one on that doomed plane...saying they loved their wives or moms before crashing into the World Trade Center.

Just look at me. I'm driving twenty-nine thousand pounds of solid truck, riding one story above ground. A thousand and fifty boxes of potato chips to deliver. I got me tires that come up to my belt. Not many women can brag on that.

Yep. There's a lot of loneliness on this job. Once, I was driving on my birthday. Now a birthday's gonna make you feel more lonely than any other day, even Christmas. And I decided, the heck with it, I'm going to have me a birthday party. So I pulled in to this new truck stop not knowing a soul with just a "Happy Birthday" streamer and a coconut cake my daughter baked and wrapped in silver paper. I looked around at all these unknown faces at the coffee bar and said, "Good morning, Vietnam." Then I started cutting the cake and handing out slices to every stranger in the place—a waitress, two state troopers, the roach exterminator, a newsboy, three truckers from Atlanta driving for Crete Carrier. We all ate cake and laughed and got to know each other. It was the best party I've ever had.

(A beat.)

Being afraid and not knowing what's going to happen next in this country, I could use more good times and plenty of comfort food. I ride by houses, buildings and they seem pretty special to me now. But I try not to dwell on fear. I know here on the road is where courageous living is—seeing people whiz by, different kinds of folks you'd never see if you were doing an ordinary job. Like that kid zooming by me on his red motorcycle. He's got him a big sticker on his bike from Frank Hawly's Drag Racing School. I've never seen anybody from there before. And that new Rail-Splitting Auto Truck Plaza coming up. If I want, I could stop there for genuine Canadian bacon along with eggs. Those poor people in Afghanistan haven't seen anything that big. Ever. Then, too, I'm looking at Lincoln Country hour after hour. What Taliban could do that? Why I feel about as close to Abe as his wife. Maybe closer. I understand Mr. and Mrs. Lincoln didn't get on too well. Not that I'm trying to be negative about the greatest man that ever was. Or about his wife, either. I was named after her.

See here. My speedometer just turned to l.3 million miles. I've only had one little fender bender in ten

years—that was in Cortland because an idiot prea-
cher from the Sunblast Christian Reformed Church
was stacking his collection envelopes with one hand
on the wheel. And once I got a ticket for going sixty-
five in a fifty-five only two days after the county
reduced the speed on us. I'm just a creature of habit.

The secret to driving a truck is not black coffee. Only
people who don't drive and see trucker movies think
that. Coffee will put you in too many restrooms. Coffee
slows you down. Gum is crucial. You chew hard and
it's like exercising while you're sitting.

See the old geezer behind me? He's slipstreaming on
me—following too close so he can get gas mileage by
tailgating me, which breaks the wind resistance. I can't
get mad at him. Not when he's flying an American flag.

Look at that girl. Just driving ever so sweetly on
cruise control with a can of beer between her legs. I
ever catch my girls doing that...

But you see American spirit everywhere on the road
these days; flags a story high flapping on the top of
cars, flag scarves on dogs who sit up real nice and tall
in the back seat, bikers in flag t-shirts. Just yester-
day I seen me what looked like two pumpkins going
to market with Barbara Bush pearls hanging down
them. You get observant on this job.

Sometimes…I look out there and I have to ask myself…are all these people going someplace to hide? Are they moving a little faster than usual because of 9-11? Is all this traffic just getting thicker 'n thicker 'cause people are afraid and on the move?

I don't know where the hands of the Doomsday Clock are right now. I know the clock is supposed to symbolize nuclear danger, and the terrorists could be getting nuclear material. The clock's earliest setting was seventeen minutes to midnight in 1991. Just before September 11th, it was set at nine minutes to midnight. How many minutes have we lost?

I won't deny that I get a little jittery now and then. Maybe that's why after a while everything begins to look fragile: Libertyville with its Tad's Caramel Corn, Woodbine Village and Four Score Elementary, Harvey's New Salem Burgers, Oswego's Emancipation Proclamation Meat Masters, Cortland's Stove Pipe Hat Body Piercing, Genoa's Todd Pancakes. And me, taking my federally regulated two-hour rest stop. Two hours by two hours. Yet there's no way I can forget that when I was a kid, my first Barbie Doll came with a sports car. Driving is in my blood. And I steady myself thinking of Old Abe. How the times must have been just as scary when the whole country back then looked like it would break in two. And America drove through that.

(She unrolls a string to let a kite fly out the truck window.)

Green Gold

CHARACTER: Patoo, Caribbean woman, age late 30-something.

PLACE: Potters Cay Dock Airport

*(At rise: **Patoo** is carrying a traveling bag and a basket of fresh fruit.)*

PATOO

Gate 4, gate 4.

(She finds the gate and stops.)

What? Of course that ticket's for Nassau. I know Nassau's only twenty minutes away, but it be good as any ticket to Montego Bay.

(A beat as she listens to the gate man.)

Yes, yes, I know about September eleven in Nova York. You take all the care you want to look me over. Use that black wand t'ing up my side and down the other. I'm no sky-jacker. I get along with everybody. I don't care if you from Kingston, Rome, Nova York,

Jo'Burg, Afghan any which way, I accept you iffing you don't pass off bad checks, don't tries to poison me, put pepper in my eyes, or if you don't shake my hand with a gun.

(She walks through the boarding gate, pauses, then puts down her bag and talks to the audience as a fellow traveler.)

I'm Patoo. My mama named me that. Means "night owl." 'Cause I can see anything. But eyes no good up there in the sky. Might as well be blind if the Taliban take over the plane cause everybody's going down— them that see and them that don't see.

(A beat.)

I sure don't want to get on, even though it be just twenty minutes to Nassau. But when the mailboat came in this morning to Potters Cay Dock saying my daughter went to the hospital to have her baby, I got no choice.

(A beat.)

She needs me. She's had enough fright. Her husband, Percy, was in Nova York when them towers came down. Yes, yes, he was there for sure. Percy always goes there. He's a supplier for wicker furniture and be talking to the manager of this Millennium Hotel on Church Street...when metal started to fly through the air like loogaroos and duppies…but it be hunks of that South Tower hitting the building. I'm thinking somet'ing nice sounding like Church Street should be safe as Potters Cay Dock.

(A beat.)

Potters Cay Dock? I was born here. My child Toola was born here. My husband Rexford Henry died here in the hurricane of 1992. Lotta people think Potter's Cay Dock just bush…not my fault that…but with the terrorists all round, maybe bush is better. Maybe people should tour the bush now and forget big fancy places…like you nobody if you don't go to Jamaica. I know people they address their letters to Nassau, Jamaica, Barbados, Jamaica, Martinique, Jamaica. Like there's no other island in the world but Jamaica.

(A beat.)

What is this at all? The plane leaving on time? Guess everybody came early and ready with the war going on.

(She hands her bag to the metal detector operator and watches him throw her bag around.)

Buccaneer, don't you throw my things upside down like that. I got a jar of beef balls inside. You want to spill coconut oil on my clean white blouse and skirt? You want to ruin the new baby blanket in there from One Bay Street?

(A beat.)

Check for knives, but don't bounce that bag like it's some wild donkey jumping up against a Mangrove tree.

(A beat.)

Lawd, Lawd, I hear you. I'm getting on the plane.

(She walks a short distance and sits on a chair.)

Used to be such an easy t'ing flying on an out island plane. No more. I know just where I was that day. At the fish market in Potters Cay Dock...out where the wind's so sweet...but soon I heard screaming...ordinary women taking baskets off they head and sitting down on the ground yelling...then all the market gossip stopped and it be so quiet I could hear fishnet-floats in the water. The jitney comes round the wharf and the driver with his bowler hat stops short using a screw driver to let himself out through the rusty door...and he calls out, "America's been bombed. America's been bombed."

(A beat.)

My, this seat's so small. I hardly fit.

(She sniffs.)

What's that smell? Like a dead cat under a tree.

(A beat.)

What! The plane's moving. God help everybody!

(She begins to fan herself nervously with a large banana leaf from her basket purse.)

Look at that: Hully-gully boy be sitting in front of me wearing his pointed shoes, white linen suit, pink glasses. Glad he's nobody in a turban with box cutters in his hand.

(She looks to another side of the plane.)

Just old men in tattered straw boaters and grease-stained felt hats. No wires hanging out.

(She looks to her window side.)

Child! Yes, you. In the red cricket hat sucking on cane. Your fingerprints is all over the window. You're clouding the window. These days, people have to see out… to look for things that be suspicious…maybe for other planes sent to save us.

(She points to fingerprints on the window.)

Your fingers. These are yours, too. Those are white people's. *(To the child:)* Now wipe off your mess so I can look out.

(A beat.)

No, I won't give you some pennies for the Calypso tent. Stay away from them singing fools. They smoke ganja. You stay under a Calypso tent too long and the flies will boo on you.

(A beat.)

I never let my Toola go to any Calypso trash.

(She leans back in her seat and closes her eyes for a beat and is then startled awake. She holds her stomach.)

My Lawd, that took my stomach by surprise. I don't think this plane is going to dive like that after we in the air. You think the pilot is steering all by hisself? I didn't see nobody strange go inside his cabin. We were going so smooth for a while…but as my sister always says, "Patoo, when the wind stops, then the sand flies get you."

(A beat.)

I'll just eat something to ease my stomach.

(She takes out a banana.)

I used to carry these on my head.

(She begins eating the banana.)

Me and my daughter, Toola. "Headers," they called us.
A stem of bananas on our head. We'd line up along
side the dock to load the cargo ships.

(She holds out a stem of bananas from her basket.)

Each banana is a finger. A cluster of them is a hand.
Toola and me, we walked all day in the sun. Our
brains hurt. My Toola, she was only twelve years old,
and we had to keep walking 'cause by the end of the
day, we'd carry all them green bananas through five
doors in the ship's topside. My Toola, she called them
green gold. She'd say, "Mama, we're just carrying
green gold."

(A beat.)

What's that! They put on the turbulence sign. Lawdy.
Lawdy. This plane is acting up. I'll just think of my
Toola when she was so little…when she stepped so
dainty along the dock…bananas on her head…fan-
ning her little breasts like the flutter of a mountain
bird. Just thinking of that cools me. Oh, her little face
is stuck in the baby of my eye.

(A beat.)

Ahhhhh. The plane is smooth now, thank the Lawd. I most thought we were gone.

(A beat.)

Oh, I tell you, hard as them banana days were, I pine for walking beside my daughter all day long.

(A beat.)

What's that pilot saying? We're landing? Lawd, hope no Afghan tinkered with the tires.

(A beat.)

It's not myself dying that frightens me. It's my thoughts dying. Who would remember my Toola...her walking beside me all day long...green gold on her head. *(She talks to the boy next to her:)* Boy, move over some so I can see out the window.

(A beat.)

Sure enough. There's Nassau down below. I see clumps of gru gru palms. Plants like wigs of green hair. Your feet don't swell up down there like they swollen with famine-dropsy the way feet do in Montego Bay.

(She braces herself in her seat for the landing. Her body jerks to a stop as the plane lands.)

Safe. I can feel the ground. Happy for trut to see my Toola. *(She gathers up her things to leave the plane. To the audience:)* You come to Potters Cay Dock, darlin', we'll drink fever-grass tea on the trade wind side of my porch.

(She stands and picks up her basket to exit the plane.)

If something has to get you, then I hope it be zombies. The hurricane that killed Rexford Henry was bad luck. The World Trade Towers coming down was bad luck. Bad luck be worse than spirits. You believe in zombies, you can cast them out right away. Bad luck is something harder and darker. You need the Lawd with that.

(A beat.)

I'm glad we had time to chat-chat. Bye darlin'.

Pilgrimage

CHARACTER: Cora, high school student, age 17-and-a-half

CORA

I was in first hour study hall on September 11th and had just started the topic sentence on my theme about *Othello*: "This play is an awful tragic triangle between Othello who loves Desdemona but Desdemona loves the Moor." That was my thesis statement, and I was about to add some evidence having just used the word "therefore," which Mrs. Dempsey said was a good conjunctive word, when our principal, Mr. Winterhalter, came over the PA and announced that two planes flew into the World Trade Center and all classes were dismissed until further notice. Some of the freshmen boys in the back of the room laughed and held out their arms like big 747 wings cause they thought it was a huge joke. But Janice Twombly screamed; she knew Mr. Winterhalter would rather die than crack a joke. Ever since then, I've come to think of *Othello* as even sadder than Shakespeare's movie, *Romeo and Juliet.*

When I got home, my mother had all the ironing still piled up in the laundry basket. Dad's shirts hung over the side of the basket with their damp wrinkled arms trailing on the floor while Mom watched TV and drank a can of Bud Lite. But skyscrapers had been destroyed and our country was invaded and she started mumbling that her father lived through a similar thing at Pearl Harbor. You see, mom never drinks beer before the six o'clock evening news.

When Dad came home, Mom refused to cook. She was crying and her hands were full of Kleenex. I wanted to send out for Chinese since I was anxious to see what the fortune cookies would say, but Mom felt that was disrespectful and told Dad to pick up some Quarter Pounders from McDonalds being that was more American.

Then, I saw a miracle. Right on TV. I'm drawn to miracles. And there...before my eyes...so close to the World Trade Center that was in awful smoldering ruins...was the 235-year-old church where George Washington once prayed: St. Paul's Episcopalian Chapel. In perfect condition. Not even a window broken and so close to the center of destruction that a sycamore tree right beside the chapel door was smashed to bits.

I knew I had to go to New York City even though I'd have to skip some classes that Mr. Winterhalter was probably not willing to give us off for national mourning. But I was hoping it would help my case that President Bush came on national news and asked students to get pen pals in the Islam World, because our country had no beef with the common Muslim. And getting from Larchmont, Connecticut to New York City doesn't really take that much time.

So here I am...looking at Ground Zero. People who work the ruins don't like to call it Ground Zero. Guess that sounds too impersonal, maybe even undignified. And the dust and toxins in the air are making the workers sick. A lot of them have something called the "Twin Towers cough." I met a cute guy who told me that asbestos was used for fireproofing in the north tower and now the asbestos level around here is unsafe. Mothers are even afraid to send their kids back to schools anywhere near the Site.

You can see workers looking in the l.2 million tons of rubble, with all those cranes hovering over the smoky debris. People are holding up American flags and photographs of their loved ones. Those Red Cross women are handing out tissues. See those two old people leaning on each other for support? And it's so awful hearing the constant grating sound of the heavy machines all the time...digging ...burrowing ... uncovering things—maybe a business card, or a charred piece of dress, a comb, anything that could identify the nearly three thousand dead. Not too long ago, they found a perfect desk calendar. Maybe moments before the plane struck, some man or woman was looking at it figuring out how many days there were before a kid's birthday or a wedding anniversary.

You can't help but think of the good that can come out of something as awful as this; like that kid from Ohio who sent four hundred pairs of gloves to rescue workers and even put a penny in the thumb of each glove for luck, and the citizens of Akron, Ohio, who bought a new fire truck, two ambulances, and three police vehicles for Ladder Company 163 in Woodside, Queens, which lost two firefighters.

I know some people think that an ancient astrologer named Nostradamus predicted everything that happened here way back in 1500. But this old Nostra guy also said we'd get over these dark times. And I wanna believe that more than any of his bad predictions.

Now, right up here is the church I was telling you about—St. Paul's Episcopalian Chapel. But I guess after September 11th, it's considered just about anybody's church and not just the Episcopalians', though they certainly have the first claim. The wooden steeple stood tall even though concrete fell and steel melted.

Think of it: A church 235 years old being strong enough to hold up next to all that fire and smoke. George Washington must have known right away that this place was special when he knelt in prayer here after being inaugurated as President in New York City in 1789.

After September 11th, this church became a stopping off point for the "first responders." See that iron fence along the front walk? Firefighters hung their shoes on it before they changed into their boots and charged bravely into the burning towers. As you can see, many of those men didn't return to get them back. It hurts to look at these shoes—so lonely, just waiting on the fence. My mom says that feet are the heart of a person.

(She takes off her shoes.)

That's why I'm going barefoot until I leave New York and maybe longer—in honor of the firemen.

(She puts the shoes around her neck.)

Another miracle was found near here. A letter, which was in a mail-bag on American Flight 11, floated down from the plane's explosion—the only letter to survive the crash. Some auctioneer said it's pretty valuable since he sold a letter from the Titanic for thirty-seven thousand dollars.

And speaking of money: Enough cash to fill sixty garbage bags was discovered at the Site, supposedly from Bank of America. It's funny…but all that money doesn't look so important mixed in with dust, iron, and pulverized human beings.

We started doing role-playing skits in homeroom just before I left. You know, like I'd pretend to be an Arab and Wendell LaVelle would heft an imaginary bowl of Matzo ball soup. Mrs. Dempsey calls it "Diversity Lessons." One freshman kid I know gave a dirty look to some Quick-Mart clerk he thought was carrying a prayer-rug but later found out it was just a bowling towel from the Idle Hours Bowling Alley. Some of us senior girls took to wearing scarves on our head to show support for one of our Arab foreign exchange students named Diyaa. But Mom said that was nothing new as she used to have to wear a scarf on her head every Sunday when she was a girl going to St. Margaret Mary's Church on Butterfield Avenue in Bridgeport. Now that church plays "America the Beautiful" after Mass each day.

Some people call what's going on a Holy War. I've never read the Koran, having had a hard enough time with Chaucer and *Othello*, though I'm getting used to "thou" and "thine" in my senior English class. I can't for one minute think any war can he holy. It's one of those grammar terms that Mrs. Dempsey says happens when one word contradicts another one. The way I see it, something's only holy when it stands bravely in the face of cruelty—like this chapel.

Mrs. Dempsey also said that too many people don't interpret the word *jihad* right. *Jihad*, she says, is only a war of the best of a person against the worst of that person. You know, good vs. evil. A personal thing. And when she explains it that way, even some of the guys in class stop calling up the local Lebanese Bakery to yell in the phone, "You blew up my country."

All this changes the way I go to sleep at night. Now, I have to look up at the Big Dipper before I close my eyes. If you follow miracles like I do, you can't ignore the stars. Some day, thousands of years from now, Americans will be going up in space to live. It's a simple matter of progress. We're going to be something better, more supernatural up there—without wars. Peace will be just an everyday occurrence up there.

Jenny's Email

CHARACTER: Jenny, housewife, age 29

JENNY

I have four children, all boys and close together in age. So I'm pretty busy and don't have time to keep up much. My husband, Roland, bought me a laptop for email and the Internet so I could at least stay in touch with family and friends. I keep it on our pink marble-lite counter top in the kitchen, which is handy for me because I can communicate with mom and my sister and old college buddies in-between cooking burgers and baking wieners-in-a-blanket or while the kids are at pre-school or down for a nap.

On September 11th, we were all up early as usual. Roland works at the Snow Creek Accounting Office on Snow Creek Avenue here in Fargo, North Dakota, so he was out the door by 7 a.m. By eight o'clock, the van had come to take Joey and Bobby to pre-school. That left Jimmy eating corn flakes and spreading soggy lines in the shape of a tree on our kitchen table that Roland had just refinished over the course of ten weekends. The baby, who we call Clanker because he's never quiet even when he's sleeping, was sitting in his play pen, hiccuping and banging a wooden spoon on the mesh frame.

I always email Roland at exactly 9:30 a.m. because that's when he breaks for coffee and that's when I am down to only two kids and can open the refrig to see what I need for him to bring home from the supermarket.

One good thing about a laptop is you can lie on the couch and put it on your belly along with a twelve-and-a-half-month-old that you're patting for hiccups. I booted up with one hand and jiggled Clanker with the other, his wooden spoon tangled in my hair. I didn't even have time to check the refrig, but I knew we always need milk so I was getting ready to type a milk-message when I saw an email from Roland with the tag, "Urgent." When I called it up, some of the words were garbled and misspelled, something Roland never does, "Jenny, take take kids to your mothers immediately. Something torrible has happened."

My mother lives in Grand Forks, which is not a quick easy drive with four kids in the back seat of the car. But besides that, Roland took our only car to work. So I put Clanker back in the play pen, poured more corn flakes into Jimmy's Cookie-Monster bowl, and emailed Roland with my own urgent message, "Roland, what is going on? I can't take the kids anywhere. You have the car." And Roland answered in bold face caps, "BE HOME IN 20 MINUTES."

When Roland came bursting into the house, having picked up Joey and Bobby from pre-school on the way, he told me the news about the World Trade Center and the Pentagon. All we could do was sit on the sofa and hold on to all our four kids. Even Clanker recognized the fear we were feeling. For the only time in the twelve and a half months of his life, Clanker was quiet.

I didn't see any need to evacuate, but Roland said Fargo was famous because of the movie *Fargo*. The Taliban forbid movies in Afghanistan and maybe they would use us as their next target. But my mother called us on her cell phone and said she was on her way to our house. So there was nothing we could do but stay put and look at TV to see President Bush in a room full of second graders in Sarasota. It was the only time in history that a camera was turned on a President at the exact moment when he heard his country was attacked.

These days after 9-11, we stay close to home. A lot of our neighbors call it *cocooning*. I call it…a rainy-day mindset. Roland doesn't even want to go back to the office after dinner, something he usually does two nights a week so his work won't pile up. Now…he just, well, lets it all pile up. He pitches in even more than ever at home. He always did help out, of course, because he joined the Marines after high school for the GI Bill and knows how to clean. Ex-Marines wash diapers, iron their shirts, and swab corn flakes off the deck without being asked.

I heard Laura Bush on the radio when she took over the President's radio address in November. It was the first time a First Lady ever delivered the traditional weekly presidential radio spot—taking the President's place. I always turn on the radio now for Clanker and Jimmy when their brothers leave for school. They're still a little timid and fearful, even after so many days have gone by. I can't help but remember the first line of that short story by Stephen Crane called *The Open Boat*, which I read in college. With men lost at sea, bouncing around the ocean in a small lifeboat, Crane tells us, "None of them knew the color of the sky." And that's the way it is now, when high alerts are issued all the time for possible attacks. None of us know the color of the sky.

Anyway, I was glad Laura Bush talked about the cruel treatment of children in Afghanistan under the Taliban. I look at my own boys...and it makes me very sad to think that any child has to starve. How long would my Clanker be able to live his clanking life just eating wild grass and carrots?

There's an old birthday invitation still on our refrig. It was sent to our oldest, Joey, from one of his little friends at pre-school. It reads, "September 11th is my birthday. Don't forget the date."

I still watch *Sesame Street* with my children, and we see Elmo visit a New York firehouse to learn about how they work.

The boys and I were very saddened by the starving old lion, Marjan, at the Kabul Zoo. His toothless, one-eyed face flashed across the world in newspapers and TV news reports. This was no simple creature from *Sesame Street*, and my boys knew it. Here was a lion disfigured by grenade and bomb attacks. This pathetic creature suffered as his people had. Joey and Bobby emptied their piggy banks and sent a total of twelve dollars and fifteen cents to the Kabul Zoo. Jimmy included a box of corn flakes. Clanker tossed in his wooden spoon.

We play a lot of cards and board games together these days. I just bought the current Trivial Pursuit. My husband and I like to play when the kids are in bed. There are 4,800 new questions, six new categories. But the box top assures Roland and me that there are no questions about 9-11. September 11th is not a trivial subject.

Daisies

CHARACTER: Captain Alley Sand, U.S. Army officer, age
32

(At rise: She holds a bouquet of daisies.)

ALLEY SAND

There's so much talk about the World Trade Center
that people tend to forget the tragedy of the Pentagon.
Not that I want to make a contest between the Towers
and what I went through.

9:43 a.m., September 11th, American's flight 77 crashed
into our citadel, collapsing one of the five sides and
making a huge gory six-story hole.

Rumsfeld, Secretary of State, felt the Pentagon shake.

The air space over D.C. is known as "Class B." No air-
craft can fly without permission and a working
transponder. I initially assumed it was an earth-
quake. Or a gas explosion. What I didn't know was
that a terrorist pilot turned 270 degrees to the right
on his route to Los Angeles and began a suicidal
southwest course directly in our path, dipping under

radar and going full throttle, shearing off trees and plunging into the side of the building killing 125 of my colleagues. And 64 passengers on the jet.

I smelled electrical fire right away. I double-timed it out of my office to the smoky corridor that ran into a blackened hallway. A three-star General was talking to a copter pilot on a satellite phone. I began to cough and some Major behind me took my arm and helped me along a dark hall. I had time to pull along a stunned woman frozen in fright, holding a federal green file folder as if it were a shield protecting her. The Major picked up a man who had fallen and jammed him up against my back as we all shoved forward in a mass.

Civilian typists and file clerks helped evacuate the terrified and wounded like experts, waving people to the stairwell and guiding them down concrete steps. A Sergeant carried a bleeding man on his back, his Class-A cap stanching blood on the man's chest. Two Lieutenants made a human stretcher with their arms, moving a woman through the halls face down, shielding her with their shoulders as running people bumped past.

Outside was a crater, a thirty-five-foot area across five floors, where the plane hit and entered in the wedge between two corridors, collapsing the outermost ring. Fire and smoke swirled up into a tornado of rage. The only positive thing I can say is that the terrorists hit the only part of the Pentagon that had actually been renovated to withstand attack. The plane was slowed down somewhat and the explosion was reduced a little. But damage was nevertheless fierce, with fire fed by twenty thousand gallons of jet fuel that cracked concrete.

I've seen a lot of strange sights in my life, having been in service since the age of twenty-one, when I got my commission after graduating from the University of Illinois. I was shipped right over to Desert Storm at the beginning of my career, so I know the battlefield. But this was something different. The front line was America's *front yard*. I was able to understand that old World War II story my father told me about an American so enraged by Pearl Harbor that he got an ax and chopped down a Washington, D.C. cherry tree given to America by the government of Japan.

But I'm no stranger to this enemy. I fought them before.

A woman soldier like me is a real oddity to people in Iraq or Afghan. When I was in Saudi, they wanted to know if I was a queen or something—like an ordinary woman couldn't be an officer on her own, like only men could be officers. Well, I once read Qaddafi's Green Book (green being the color of Islam) to get a feel of those people and I want you to know that it was all scatter-shot thoughts. Take it from me, he's more ramble than Rambo.

I had to socialize in a lot of goat-hair tents. A good officer fraternizes with the coalition troops and they liked me because my name is a little Arab-ish...you know...Alley...Sand. So when we were off duty, Captain Yamn or Major Ahmed and I would go to the Babel Movie House in Rafhah and see Bruce Lee movies when the SCUDs were slow. Later I'd go to their little cinder block family house and their wives would serve dates and camel's milk. Many times dinner was a whole sheep stretched out on a bed of rice.

At the beginning of the war on terrorism, I was assigned to an MC-130 Cargo Plane dropping Daisy Cutters on caves in Afghanistan. The Daisy Cutter leaves a circular pattern where it hits—thus its name. But unlike a daisy, it's the size of a small car and incinerates everything within 600 yards with 12,600 pounds of explosives. We used it in the Gulf War to clear minefields. Once the entire staff of an Iraqi battalion surrendered when a Daisy was dropped near their camp because they thought we would drop it on them next.

Our MC-130 carries the Daisy on a moveable platform. When we get about six thousand feet, we open the back of the plane and she's dragged out by a parachute. Then she's released from the chute by a static-release line. A second parachute opens and a thirty-eight-inch fuse detonates the Daisy about three or four feet from the ground. It's a marvel of technology and raw recruits ought to see it right away—this weapon is not the ex-cathedra type of rote-firing that the Army so often seems to favor. And of course that's why the Pentagon changed the color of humanitarian food packets. Unexploded cluster bombs are yellow. The new food packets will be blue.

I was there when we took Mazar-i-Sharif, helped by a group of rag-tag Opposition Forces. Well, I wasn't technically there but hovering in a Cobra Copter overseeing a pincer attack while lending support fire. It was gratifying watching the Taliban fall back against the northern slope of the Hindu Kush. I remember Orville Wright once said a long time ago that the airplane would give eyes to the armies, and the armies with the eyes would win the war.

Ask any of our Afghan support soldiers what kind of weapons they want from us and they'll say...*shoes*. I'd see our turban-allies in bare feet riding their camels up against Taliban tanks. But that tells you what kind of primitive military support we have.

Mazar-i-Sharif isn't much of a prize. Worse than any town you'd likely ever see even in turban countries. After the Taliban were gone, a bunch of Rebels carrying Kalashnikov rifles and three of us Americans carrying suitcases full of cash all marched into the city that was now flying the green, white, and black flags of the Alliance. A native man immediately shaved his beard—his towel draped over a blown-apart donkey. Balloon vendors raced on their bicycles to the market place. Women uncovered their faces. One old man sold pictures of Indian movie stars in bikini-saris along-side kids playing in a mound of 122-millimeter shells. Some weird Afghan singer called Naim Pupal sang on the sound system of many shops. A one-legged man hobbled down a tank trail with a second-hand TV strapped to his back. Two little girls, with red balls of yarn in their hair, gave me flowers. It was like Ike liberating Paris. Somewhere in a cave, Sheik Osama must have been furious.

The President gave the First Lady tulips for Valentine's Day, and the Tootsie Roll people sent us one million pieces of the candy for our Valentine's Day—little Tootsie Roll runts with special red-white-blue wrappers. Chewing one of those, I felt historic. Those candies were part of World War I rations…and were also dropped to starving troops in the Korean Conflict. I was munching one of the chocolate midges when I saw a mob of Afghans swarming down the street. At first I was afraid that the stampede would trample me. But the mob ran right by and straight to a broken down cinema with two hundred splintering wooden seats. The film playing was *Elan*, an Indian action flick. The Afghans couldn't even understand the language. But they didn't care. One old man, who bragged he learned English from tapes, said that the people dying in the film weren't realistic. Being an

Afghan, he'd seen a lot of dying and up on the screen wasn't real death. Still, he was happy to pay three thousand Afghanis—about seventy cents—to get in because he hadn't seen a movie in six years.

(A silent beat. She begins to smell the daisies.)

The daisy. Poets call these…"day's eye." They're nearly a weed. But hardy. They even make a good flower wine. Good lineage, too. During the time of the troubadours, daisies were on their coat-of-arms. And as Alice in wonderland knows, daisies can talk. These would probably quote Machiavelli: "All armed prophets won and the unarmed perished." Yes, sir, daisies can talk.

(She puts one daisy behind her ear as the lights slowly go down.)

War Dogs

CHARACTER: Fala, Franklin Delano Roosevelt's pet dog

(At rise: We see an actor in a black body suit with black Scottie ears wearing a World War II Navy cape and holding a cigarette holder sitting in a 1940s wheelchair.)

FALA

Do you think…that you people are the first to ever experience an attack on the homeland? Our country was hit before. In 1941. At Pearl. Remember?

*(**Fala** stands.)*

Name's Fala—Franklin D. Roosevelt's dog. I was sleeping by this very wheelchair when Franklin took the call about Pearl Harbor. He was drinking tea and dropped the cup on the floor. He stared at all those splinters of glass like it was his country that had just broken apart. Then he leaned over wanting to put back the pieces, but of course that was impossible. He had polio, you know. There was even a canvas chute outside my FDR's bedroom window so he could slide down to the lawn in case of fire.

We were just as frightened and confused as you folks are right now. But sometimes I think people tend to panic more than dogs. Like I heard there's a move today to change the name of the Afghan Hound Club of America due to the war in Afghanistan. Luckily, the club refused; Afghan Hounds are by nature pacifists.

Don't look so startled…like you're seeing a ghost. You all seem to think the dead sit around on clouds up in heaven. Well, I'm here to tell you that's not true—maybe for people, but not for dogs. I've never left America. I'm still everywhere in the streets. To be dead is to be more alive in a hundred thousand different ways; ways that were dead to you when you were alive, like having eyes that hear and think and ears that see and speak.

My brothers are true heroes—right there at Ground Zero on September 11th. There was this blind man at his desk on the 78th floor of the World Trade Center. His dog, Roselle, led him and his colleagues down to the first floor. As Tower Two collapsed, Roselle continued to lead her companion and a trail of co-workers all the way to the river and safety.

My kind worked side by side with all the first responders at the Site—like Porkchop, a two-year-old Australian Shepherd who wore bandages and leather booties to protect his feet. Porkchop worked a twelve-hour shift, sniffing and rummaging around in the rubble. At first he discovered survivors…then he unearthed clothing or personal papers, and then… human remains. A dog's eyes are just as sensitive as yours, and Porkchop and his buddies' eyes were constantly burning from all the acrid dust and methane gas bubbling up from the mud. Sometimes they limped from getting their legs or paws crimped in all the debris. Those mutts worked without surgical masks and were gagged by smoke and ash inhalation.

I don't mean to belittle the human race, but it's pure fact that we dogs can smell better than any of you. That's why we're so valuable. Our nose makes up a large percentage of our brain space. We got 230 million scent receptors and you folks have only ten million.

I hate to brag, but dogs work on Pavlovian conditioning, a kind of classy psychology that some of you who went to college might know about. We are trained to associate specific odors with a reward. If we smell a briefcase under bricks and steel, for example, we know we're going to get a treat from our owner.

Added to the horror of what happened at the Twin Towers, we heard that the Taliban experimented with nerve gas on us dogs. Psychologists say that notorious killers often vent their fury on animals. That made rescue-canines even more eager to do their job.

Within hours of the tragedy, canines were there and sniffing out many of the wounded, even as glass and steel sliced into their paws. A couple of my brothers nearly smothered after falling into a quicksand of ash. Many got cuts on their bellies and backs from snaking through hot twisted steel. A special Mash Unit for dogs, a four-foot long bus with operating room and x-ray equipment, was set up at Ground Zero. Heroes, all of the Ground Zero dogs: Cowboy, a Border Collie; Nero, a German Shepherd; Gus, a yellow Lab from Tennessee; Bella, a Border Collie from L.A.; and so many more. The Westminster Kennel Club Dog Show gave the 9-11 canines a special salute...and when they padded into Madison Square Garden with their handlers, there was a standing human ovation.

I'll be the first to say that a lot of non-canines put their lives on the line to save pets trapped in buildings left behind because of immediate evacuations. A teacher at Trinity pre-school helped save the school rabbit and mascot, Peter. And a human from the ASPCA climbed thirty-eight stories, broke down a door, and hacked his way through rubble to retrieve a gecko. He also liberated a snake on the 27th floor.

My kind suffered stress as bad as humans did. When they couldn't find anybody, they began to whine and scratch themselves restlessly. Their trainers had to provide exercises to help relieve the frustration and anxiety over their defeat of not saving lives. One of my brothers went wildly happy on discovering a man in some mud bubbles. Sadly, it wasn't a real man but a bronze figure by Rodin called *The Three Shades* that once stood in the offices of Cantor Fitzgerald at the World Trade Center's North Tower. The sculpture, now headless and footless, was taken off to a landfill on Staten Island and my brother had to cope with his depression. He was trained to find the living—not cadavers and statues. The Ralston Purina Company, I'm happy to say, is funding a hundred thousand dollar, three-year study to research distress suffered by search and rescue dogs at the site.

My brothers also did therapy for people who lost loved ones. Therapy dogs help grieving people. Petting an animal can bring down your blood pressure.

(A beat.)

I'm not particularly partial to cats, but I have to admire a lady named Cleo, a feline who worked her tail off in comforting humans since September 11th.

I guess that's why I've come back. Consider me a historical therapy dog come to comfort you. I just want you to know that we went through really terrible times in the past. And we made it.

Oh, when we heard about Pearl...I won't lie to you and say we weren't scared. 'Cause we were. All of us. Like most of you right now.

Black air raid curtains were on our White House windows. A gas mask hung on my FDR's wheelchair. I was even made an honorary private in the United States Army.

I was proud of my Franklin when he approved all the paper work for the War Dog Platoons. There were scout dogs in W-W-II who went in advance on patrols. Messenger dogs. Mine dogs who detected explosives. And they were real soldiers just like men.

Yes, my President knew the importance of dogs. I was one of his closest associates, after all. I was always around giving him as much comfort, love, and assistance as I could...like my brothers are doing today after September 11th. Why, I was on Franklin's lap when he gave this country very good advice. You people today need to hear it: "This great nation will endure as it has endured, will revive and will prosper. We have nothing to fear but fear itself."

And I guess that is what I want you to remember. People have an annoying way of forgetting. We came through those dark times. And you'll come through, too.

(*Fala* sits back in the wheelchair and turns the chair around. We see his back as he holds out his signature cigarette holder and pops on a fedora hat between his Scottie ears.)

(At the end of the last monologue, the lights go black. Then the lights come up on the actors as they stand holding each other up (for moral support) so that they are looking like the famous Iwo Jima picture. **Terry's Father**—standing on the highest level raising high the hair brush—is held up at a slant by the other characters, who hold their individual props high as well.)

(Black out.)